A Scent of Sweden

by
Kristina Kisthinios

prisma

[P

Prisma
Besöksadress: Tryckerigatan 4
Box 2052
103 12 Stockholm

www.prismabok.se

Prisma is a division of
Norstedts Förlagsgrupp AB,
founded in 1823

© Prisma 2000, 2004
First edition 1999
Second edition 2000
Third edition, fourth printing 2007
Author: Kristina Kisthinios

Background Information: The Swedish Institute and Positive Sweden
Design: Maria Rosberg and Dag Ståleker
Cover Design: Norma Communication
Translation Support: Mark Wells AB and Julian Baldwin

Printed by Fälth & Hässler, Värnamo 2007
ISBN 978-91-518-4276-9

Contents

General Facts about Sweden....... 5
   Geology 5
   Climate......................... 5
   Population 6
   Form of Government 6
   Religion........................ 7
   Trade and Industry 7
   Education 8

Curious Facts.................... 9

The Nobel Prize 11

Facts for the Visitor............. 12

Historical Highlights............. 14
   Viking Crusades 14
   Founding a Kingdom 14
      Saint Bridget 16
   The Hansa Period 17
   Gustav Vasa 17
   Gustav II Adolf................ 17
      Queen Christina 18
   Era of Liberty................. 18
   Gustav III.................... 19
   Period of Peace................. 20
   From Poor to Wealthy............ 20
   The Welfare State 20

A Creative Spirit................ 23

Popular Profiles.................. 45

Swedish Traditions.............. 47
   Events of Easter 47
   Walpurgis Eve and Mayday 49
   Midsummer Merrymaking 51
   Crayfish under the Moon 52
   Early Autumn Delicacies 54
   St. Martin's Goose Eve............. 56
   Lucia, Lusse Cats and Starboys 59
   The Tale of Christmas 60

A Map of Sweden 64

The Provinces of Sweden 66
   Southern Sweden 66
   Central Sweden 71
      The Water Province............... 71
      Magical Värmland................ 72
      Fishing and Seaside Resorts......... 74
      The Heart of Sweden.............. 75
   Idyllic Islands 76
   Northern Sweden 79
      Popular Pastimes................. 81
      Exploiting Ore 81
      Trekking 81
      Norrbotten 82
   Stockholm 84

Recipes.......................... 88

General Facts about Sweden

PHOTO: CD BILDARKIV

Population: 9 million
Area: 450,000 km²
Capital: Stockholm
Language: Swedish
    (Germanic roots)
Religion: Evangelical-Lutheran
Currency: Krona (SEK)

Geology

From a geological point of view Sweden is a very old country. In many places the bedrock is a primary one and contains the oldest kinds of rocks in existence. These are the remains of enormous mountain chains, which have eroded over time.

Sweden has experienced four ice ages. These have produced a varying landscape, from the flat south (which was covered by water) to the mountainous north, with Kebnekaise (2,111 m) as its highest peak.

The country is the third largest in Western Europe.

Climate

Throughout the entire country, Sweden's climate is about eight degrees Celsius warmer than most other countries at the same latitude. This is because of the proximity to the warm Gulf Stream in the Atlantic Ocean.

The greatest annual rainfall occurs in the mountainous regions – more than 1,000 mm. Sweden is situated in the northernmost part of the temperate climatic belt. The highest record temperature is 39° C in Ultuna and the lowest, –53° C, was measured in Vuogatjolme. Sweden has very distinct seasons, with cold winters, blossoming springs and reasonably warm summers.

Population

At the beginning of the 20th century Sweden's population was 5.1 million, in 1950 seven million and in 2002 almost nine million. The three largest cities are Stockholm, Gothenburg and Malmö, and the most sparsely populated areas are the northern provinces of Jämtland and Norrbotten with an average of only three inhabitants per square kilometre. Swedish women give birth to an average of 1.5 children and people live comparatively long lives – an average of 77 years for men and 82 for women (2002). The Samis (Lapps) are an ethnic minority group within Swedish society. There are about 15,000 Sami and about 1,000 still live according to tradition, herding reindeer. Through immigration, Sweden has become a multicultural country with about 476,000 foreign citizens. Today, 1.1 million Swedish citizens have foreign roots.

Form of Government

Sweden is a constitutional monarchy with a democratically elected government. Through representatives, the Swedes decide matters of national concern and this is applied through a parliament where the government must have the confidence of the parliament members. Elections are held every four years and the government consists of the Prime Minister and a number of cabinet ministers.

The reigning monarch is considered to be the Head of State but in reality he/she has purely symbolic and representative functions. The monarch must disclose private income and pay taxes just as all other Swedish citizens. In addition, the Royal Family are entitled to vote but do not exercise this right according to practice.

Monarchy

King Carl XVI Gustaf acceded the throne in 1973, only 27 years old. He took as his motto: "For Sweden – in keeping with the times." The King married Silvia Renate Sommerlath in 1976, making her the Queen of Sweden. They have three children: Crown Princess Victoria (1977), Prince Carl Philip (1979) and Princess Madeleine (1982).

The Royal Family resides in Drottningholm Palace in the outskirts of Stockholm.

Religion

In comparison to the 19th century, Swedish society is now largely secularised. 82 % of the population belong to the Christian, Evangelical-Lutheran church (which no longer is referred to as the State church). The church is separated into 13 dioceses, each led by a bishop. The bishop in Uppsala is referred to as the Arch-bishop and is the leader of the church. In Sweden there is total freedom of religion, which means that it is possible to practise any other religion.

Sweden is situated in northern Europe.

Trade and Industry

A hundred years ago 75 % of the population were engaged in agriculture. Today this figure is down to 3 %, showing the nation's transformation from an agricultural country to an industrial nation. The forests have been of major importance to Sweden, just as Sweden's other main resource, iron ore, has laid the foundation for the iron and steel industry. At the beginning of the 1970's Sweden was the greatest iron ore exporter in the world but by today this trade has decreased.

Sweden's economy is highly dependent on its trading relationships with other countries – about half of industrial production goes abroad (mainly to Germany and Great Britain). In the field of imports also, Europe is the most important trading partner. Sweden's main exports are paper, electronic and computer equipment, music, motor vehicles, machinery, chemical products, foods, iron and steel.

In December 1994, Sweden joined the European Community, but is otherwise considered a neutral country (not part of NATO for example).

Education

In 1842 a law was passed which made schooling obligatory for all Swedish children. Today this elementary education consists of nine years compulsory schooling and is the responsibility of each municipality.

After the compulsory school a three-year high school education is available with a variety of subjects on offer. A high school education is regarded as almost a necessity in Sweden as the standard of education required for all types of work has increased.

Finally, there are the universities, which offer a wide range of theoretical and practical courses. The oldest ones are situated in Uppsala and Lund. After approximately three years of study a student will attain his/her bachelor's degree.

The Royal Crown Jewels.

Curious Facts

A law called "Allemansrätten", i.e. the legal right to enter private land, is built on the notion that the land belongs to everyone. You may wander freely virtually anywhere without any special permission.

Sweden has eight climate zones.

The country is the world's third largest exporter of popular music.

The trend-sensitive Swedish market is widely used as a test ground by multinationals in the development of new products.

The first country in the world to introduce "freedom of press" (1776).

Largest annual ski race in the world, more than 14,000 skiers participate in the Vasa Marathon.

World's highest recycling and retrieval investment per capita; 92 % of all aluminium cans recycled.

Sweden reportedly has the largest number of amateur choirs per capita in the world.

In Sweden, more cookery books are published per capita than in any other country!

There are 50,000 square meters of land at each Swede's "disposal".

More telephone lines per capita than any other country in the world; every fourth Swede has a mobile phone.

Equal opportunity country, almost 50 % of MPs and government ministers are women.

Garage rock is the latest musical genre to be hit by the "Swedish invasion". The biggest name is The Hives, sometimes called "the new Rolling Stones".

More than one third of the elks in Europe is found in the forests of Sweden.

The Nobel Prize award ceremony in Stockholm.

Swedish Nobel Prize Winners
Physics: 1912 Gustaf Dalén, 1924 Manne Siegbahn, 1970 Hannes Alfvén (shared), 1981 Kai Siegbahn (shared)
Chemistry: 1903 Svante Arrhenius, 1926 The Svedberg, 1929 Hans von Euler-Chelpin (shared), 1948 Arne Tiselius
Medicine or Physiology: 1911 Allvar Gullstrand, 1955 Hugo Theorell, 1967 Ragnar Granit, 1970 Ulf von Euler (shared), 1981 Torsten Wiesel, 1982 Sune Bergström (shared), 1982 Bengt Samuelsson (shared)
Literature: 1909 Selma Lagerlöf, 1916 Verner von Heidenstam, 1931 Erik Axel Karlfeldt, 1951 Pär Lagerkvist, 1966 Nelly Sachs (shared), 1974 Eyvind Johnson and Harry Martinson (shared)
Peace Price: 1908 Klas Pontus Arnoldson, 1921 Hjalmar Branting (shared), 1930 Nathan Söderblom, 1961 Dag Hammarskjöld, 1982 Alva Myrdal (shared)
Economics: 1974 Gunnar Myrdal (shared), 1977 Bertil Ohlin

The Nobel Prize

In his will of 1896, the famous inventor of dynamite, Alfred Nobel, stipulated that the income from his estate should be divided into five equal parts. They should be distributed "in the form of prizes to those who, during the preceding year, have conferred the greatest benefit to mankind". Today, the Nobel Prize is awarded in the fields of Physics, Chemistry, Physiology/ Medicine, Literature, Economics and Peace. Initially there were five prizes, but in 1968 the separately funded prize for Economics was added.

There are six special Nobel committees attached to the prize-awarding bodies and the prizes are awarded at a ceremony held in the Stockholm Concert Hall on December 10, the anniversary of Nobel's death. At this event His Majesty the King of Sweden hands each prize winner a diploma, a medal and a document confirming the prize amount. The award ceremony is followed by a banquet in the Blue Hall of the Stockholm City Hall. The Peace Prize presentation takes place in Oslo the same day and is presented by the Chairman of the Norwegian Nobel Committee. These awards are recognized as the world's highest civic honours and, in 2003, were estimated to have a value of some SEK 10 million per prize.

The Nobel Foundation is a private institution, established in 1900 on the basis of Alfred Nobel's will and the statutes approved under the provisions of the will. The Foundation is entrusted with protecting the common interest of the prize-awarding bodies named in the will, as well as representing the Nobel institutions externally. This includes informal activities as well as arrangements related to the presentation of the Nobel Prizes. The foundation is also responsible for managing the funds in such a way as to preserve its financial base, while guaranteeing the independence of the prize-awarding bodies when they select the laureates.

Facts for the Visitor

Money

The unit of currency is the "krona" (SEK), which is divided into 100 "öre". Currency can be exchanged at banks and special exchange offices.

Banks

Banks can be found in most communities and are usually open Monday to Friday from 10 am to 3 pm. Most credit cards and traveller's cheques are accepted in Sweden.

Tipping

Tips and service charges are normally included on the bill, but some people still add tip at restaurants, in taxi etc. 10 % is recommended if the service has been good.

Medical Care

Medical care is available at public or private clinics. Citizens of some countries are covered by special agreements, which entitle them to reduced charges. It is advisable to arrange special insurance before you start your trip.

Emergency number

Dial 112 (SOS Alarm) for an ambulance or to call the police.

Pharmacies

Opening hours are 9 am to 6 pm on weekdays, and 9 am to 12 pm on Saturdays. In larger cities there is usually one pharmacy open in the evening and on Sundays.

Alcoholic drinks

Only weak beer can be purchased at supermarkets. Stronger beer, wine and spirits can only be purchased at the state monopoly shop "Systembolaget". The minimum age for the purchase of alcohol is 20 years.

Stamps and Telephones

Stamps can be bought – and letters sent – in places with the Postal sign outside (yellow). Telephone cards can be purchased in kiosks and grocery stores. For international telephone calls from Sweden the access code is 00.

Business hours

Office hours are often from 8 am to 5 pm and lunch commences around 12 o'clock. Shops are open from 10 am to 6 pm on weekdays, Saturdays 10 am to about 2 pm and are closed on Sundays. Some supermarkets are open on Sundays and shopping malls have extended hours.

Electricity

Power is 230v AC, 50 Hz.

Etiquette

Swedes do not have many "don'ts". *Tack* (thank you) is used very often. Many shops and banks have a queuing system. You take a number from a ticket-issuing machine and when your number is called or appears on an electronic display you proceed to the counter indicated.

Bargaining is not a natural part of most day-to-day transactions.

Languages

Swedish is the official language but most Swedes speak quite good English. The younger generation sometimes speaks a third language, such as German or French.

Tourist Office

At the Tourist Office you can get free maps and brochures. The staff will answer questions about the city, events, public transport etc.

Historical Highlights

Viking Crusades

During the Viking Age, 800–1050 AD, a market expansion took place. In Sweden this was mainly directed eastwards. Many Swedish Viking expeditions set sail with the dual purposes of plunder and trade along the east coast of the Baltic Sea and via the rivers stretching deep into present-day Russia. Here they established trading stations. They travelled as far as the Black and Caspian Seas, trading with the Byzantine Empire and the Arabs.

Being a Viking usually implied being a pirate. The ancient Norwegian noun viking means piracy. The success of the Viking crusades depended mainly on their excellent ships, though the Vikings were also equipped with unusually effective weapons.

At the beginning of the Viking Age all the Scandinavian countries were still heathen. People believed in the father of all gods, Oden, the Zeus of Nordic mythology, and his son Thor. They lived in Valhalla with a multitude of gods and the female Valkyries, who greeted fallen heroes with wine.

Christianity first reached Sweden in the 9th century, around the time of the Vikings, with the missionary Ansgar, who came from the Carolingian Empire.

It was not until the 11th century that Sweden was Christianised.

Founding a Kingdom

The independent provinces of Sweden were merged into one kingdom in the year 1000. From the middle of the 12th century there was an intense struggle for power between the Sverker and Erik families, who held the crown alternately between 1160 and 1250. In 1280 King Magnus Ladulås

Raiders, traders and explorers. The Vikings used their excellent ships to get as far as North America and Asia.

passed a law, which involved the establishment of temporal nobility and feudalism. A council was also set up to advise the king, and in 1350 a single code of law was established for the whole country.

Saint Bridget – Feminist Saint

Born in 1303, Bridget (Birgitta) was a contemporary of Marco Polo and Dante. She married Ulf Gudmarsson at the age of 13 and had 8 children. When her husband died after 28 years of marriage, she dedicated the rest of her life to God. Eventually, she found that God had dictated the foundation of a "new vineyard to His Mother's glory" – a new convent and order. Bridget decided that her convent would be established in Vadstena, on the northeast side of Lake Vättern. This convent was finished after her death.

In 1350, she settled in Rome, becoming a well-known figure in ecclesiastical politics. The main political message of Bridget was the revival of Rome as the centre of Christianity.

A papal Bull approved Bridget's order, the Order of the Most Holy Saviour, in 1370, three years before her death.

Her Revelations, "Revelationes Celestes", are gathered in eight books and one supplement (about 1,400 pages altogether). After Jesus' death, Mary became both "head and queen" of the twelve apostles and the other disciples, Bridget writes. The first Christian community, in Bridget's view, was therefore a matriarchate.

Bridget died in Rome in 1373 and was canonized in 1384. She lies buried in Vadstena.

Today, there are three branches of her order.

The Hansa Period

During the 14th, 15th and 16th centuries trade increased, especially with the German towns in the Hanseatic League, and commerce flourished. Agriculture also developed with the introduction of the three-field system, however, from 1350, millions of people perished from the plague of Black Death and this led to a long period of economic decline.

Gustav Vasa – Rebel and Monarch

The kingdoms of Denmark, Norway and Sweden were united under the Danish Queen Margareta in 1389, through inheritance and family ties. This whole period was marked by conflict, which culminated in the Bloodbath of Stockholm in 1520, during which many leading Swedes were executed by the Danish king. Among those executed were the father, uncles and other relatives of the nobleman Gustav Vasa. His mother, grandmother and three sisters were thrown in jail.

A rebellion against the Danish king, lead by Gustav Vasa, spread quickly once he had persuaded his allies to join him. Gustav Vasa became king in 1521 after gaining the support of Lübeck.

Gustav Vasa's long reign had a great impact on Sweden. During this period the foundations of the Swedish state were laid. The church was turned into a national institution, its estates were confiscated and the Protestant Reformation was introduced. At the same time power was concentrated in the hands of the king and a hereditary monarchy was also introduced.

Gustav II Adolf – the Warrior King

Since the end of the union, Sweden had endeavoured to dominate the Baltic Sea, and from the 1560's onwards this led to repeated wars with Denmark. After Gustav II Adolf intervened successfully in 1630, in the Thirty Years' War, and became one of Europe's leading monarchs, Sweden defeated Denmark in two wars. These victories led to the incorporation of some previously Danish and Norwegian provinces. Finland, as well as a number of provinces in northern Germany and the present-day Baltic republics, also belonged to Sweden.

The warrior king Gustav II Adolf had great significance for world history. He saved Protestantism, limited German imperial power and made Sweden a great power. Gustav II Adolf was killed prematurely on November 6, 1632, in the battle of Lützen.

After peace in 1658, Sweden was a great power in northern Europe but it could not hold on to its power for long, because the country lacked the required resources. After the Napoleonic Wars, Sweden's frontiers became much smaller.

Queen Christina – Last Vasa Monarch
Queen Christina of Sweden (1626–1689) is mainly remembered for her cultural patronage and her unwillingness to accept the traditional feminine role of her time. She therefore declared, while still young, that she would never marry. However, she is also remembered for her controversial conversion to Catholicism and abdication from the Swedish throne in 1654. This made Christina leave Sweden for Rome, where she was connected to the court of the Roman pontiffs.

Era of Liberty

After the death of Karl XII (or Charles XII) in 1718 and the defeat in the Great Northern War, the Swedish Parliament abolished royal absolutism and placed power in the hands of Parliament. During the Era of Liberty (1719–1772) Sweden developed a form of parliamentary government, which meant that the party dominant in Parliament chose the government, which in turn was responsible to Parliament.

Gustav III – Patron of Culture

Known to later generations mainly as the Theatre King, Gustav III was raised in a French, literary environment. Through a bloodless coup in 1772 he re-established the power of the king and became the centre of that era's French-orientated cultural life. Gustav III founded the Opera, the Swedish Academy and the Academy of Music, and he was known to be a great speaker and writer.

The first period of Gustav III's reign was marked by reform, the Swedish people's dislike of unpopular laws and Gustav's extravagant lifestyle. To regain popularity, the king planned a war against Russia. The war continued to 1790 but resulted in no territorial gains.

After the war Gustav III turned his attention towards revolutionary France, but did not live long enough to realize his war plans. He was assassinated by a conspiracy of noblemen at a masked ball in 1792. Gustav III was succeeded by his son, King Gustav IV Adolf.

PHOTO: STEN VILSON/ATELJÉ SUNDAHL AB

A portrait of Gustav III, painted by Lorens Pasch in the 1780's.

Period of Peace

Domestic politics were marked by a period of calm and peace after King Gustav IV Adolf (1792–1809) lost the throne in 1809. The French marshal Jean Baptiste Bernadotte became king in 1818 as Karl XIV Johan. Bernadotte succeeded in forcing Norway into a union with Sweden in 1814. This union was peacefully dissolved in 1905 after many internal disputes.

In 1842 compulsory education was introduced, and the reigns of King Karl XIV Johan's son and grandson, Oskar I and Karl XV, saw the end of the guild system; the adoption of free trade; and finally the introduction of local self-government in 1862 and the reform of Parliament.

From Poor to Wealthy

In general terms, 18th century Sweden went through rapid cultural developments, which was influenced by its close contact with France. Overseas trade, which also developed at a rapid pace, was hit hard by the Napoleonic Wars, which led to general stagnation and economic crisis in Sweden during the first part of the 19th century. Even during the latter part of the century, Sweden was still a poor country, in which 90 % of the population earned their living from agriculture. One consequence of this situation was a substantial emigration, mainly to North America. Over one million Swedes (one out of five) emigrated between 1866 and 1914.

Industry did not begin to flourish until the 1890's. Then it developed more rapidly between 1900 and 1930, transforming Sweden into one of Europe's leading industrial nations after the Second World War.

The Welfare State

The expansion of industry took place at a very rapid rate during the 1950's and 1960's, and by the beginning of the 1970's, the swift growth in production had brought about a steep rise in living standards in Sweden. During the 1980's, economic growth was about the same as in other Western countries.

The murder of the Social Democrat Olof Palme on February 28, 1986, came as a shock to Swedish people, who had been spared from political violence for nearly 200 years. The murderer(s) were never found, in spite of numerous investigations.

After the 1991–1993 recession, the economy recovered significantly. There was a substantial growth in exports and an increased competitiveness of Swedish industry.

The Swedish economy is currently (2003) developing satisfactorily. Growth is high, the number of available jobs increasing, while inflation is low. Both public finances and the current account show pluses. Swedish economy has not been this good since the late 1960's.

Sweden is famous for its social insurance. The characteristic features are that it is universal, compulsory and designed to protect living standards. It is financed mainly via taxes and employer payroll fees.

Compared to other countries, Sweden is known for its even distribution of incomes and wealth. This is partly because of the large percentage of public sector employees – public institutions employ about one third of the labour force.

Furthermore, the high percentage of multinational companies and the country's famous innovative spirit promise a continued positive economic development of the Swedish society.

PHOTO: PER-ERIK ADAMSSON/GREATSHOTS

The city hall is one of the most majestic buildings in Stockholm.

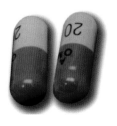  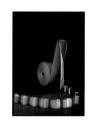

A Creative Spirit

Swedes have always been partial to inventing things. Through the centuries, these northern Europeans have developed many brilliant and important innovations to serve humanity. In the following pages we present a few of these creative thinkers and their great inventions.

The Computer Mouse

visionary Swedish invention

Håkan Lans belongs to the new generation of inventors. Among his inventions are the computer mouse, colour graphics and a navigation system that has been suggested as the new international standard.

Lans developed the computer mouse in the 1970's but it was difficult to find a manufacturer. It was even harder to find buyers.

After one year, the American company Houston Instruments had only sold forty mice. Unfortunately, Lans never applied for a patent on his idea.

Another invention, computer colour graphics, was also met with scepticism. In 1979, Lans patented the technique and after six long years IBM bought the first licence. At first, the computer companies thought that the technology was incredible, but that it lacked a market. Today, a black and white screen is considered entirely out of date.

In the 1980's Lans started thinking about his next invention. He had read about an American satellite navigation system, which, with the help of digital radio waves from satellites, could help you establish your position. Lans worked out that if he completed the system with a radio link, which sent out position reports to both users and land stations, then a new type of system could be created, indicating everyone's position. The system was called STDMA and received a patent in 1991.

The Steel Ball Bearing

smoothing industrial operations

In the year 1905 the young engineer Sven Wingquist was employed at the Gamlestaden Mills, a small textile factory in Göteborg. He had encountered some serious problems with certain machines, and to solve the problems he came up with a solution – a new ball bearing made from Swedish steel!

In order to develop Wingquist's invention, a company called AB Svenska Kullagerfabriken, in short SKF, was established in 1907. Eleven years later SKF had expanded to twelve factories and more than 12,000 employees in several countries.

Low friction with ball bearings.

Today, some 90 years later, SKF is a company of worldwide reputation for its high quality bearings. In 79 factories all over the world 227,000 bearings are produced every hour. With more than 90 per cent of its trade outside Sweden, SKF has become a truly global player in the industrial market. At the same time, SKF is one of the largest employers in Göteborg, where the company still maintains its headquarters.

For Sven Wingquist the ball bearing became a lifelong commitment. He died in 1953, at the age of 76, after having devoted almost all his life to different projects at SKF.

The Pacemaker

a life-saver for nearly forty years

Electrical impulses control the rhythm of the heart. For some people, whose impulses are deficient, the pacemaker provides these pulses.

The world's first pacemaker was produced by the company Pacesetter (Elema-Schönander AB) in October 1958. The men behind this achievement were Rune Elmqvist and Åke Senning, two of the foremost Swedish innovators of their time.

Arne Larsson was the man who gave impetus to the development of the pacemaker. He was a 43-year-old patient suffering from life-threatening sudden falls in blood pressure, which sometimes required up to thirty resuscitations a day. In 1958 Arne Larsson became the lucky recipient of the first pacemaker.

The first implanted pacemaker was as large as an ice-hockey puck and relatively simple in its construction, but

Microny, the world's smallest pacemaker. Natural size.

today it is smaller and technically advanced. Pacesetter, which today is a St. Jude Medical company, has extensively developed the pacemaker. In 1994 the AutoCapture pacemaker was introduced, Microny, weighing only 12.8 grams, the world's smallest single chamber rate-responsive pulse generator. The AutoCapture technique is revolutionary through its capacity to automatically control and secure every heartbeat. This means longer life for the pacemaker, ease of use for the doctor and lower costs for the hospitals.

Each year the pacemaker improves the quality of life for hundreds of thousands of people.

The Ericsson Story

from telegraphs to mobile phones

Sweden has got most mobile phones per capita in the world.

Lars Magnus Ericsson had worked as a farmer, smith, railway worker and repairman, when he received a scholarship in 1876 for an education in electro-technology. At the time of receiving the scholarship, Ericsson was working in a tool and telegraph workshop. Later, he opened a workshop of his own.

During 1876 Ericsson had been working mainly on telegraphs, but when he heard of Bell's brilliant invention he came up with the idea of producing telephones himself. Subsequently Ericsson started developing equipment for entire telephone networks. In 1884 he developed the first desk telephone with a separate handheld microphone and two years later he produced the first automatic telephone switchboards.

By the end of the century the company had already exported telephones to Russia, Norway, England and many other countries. In 1903, when Ericsson left his management position, the company had grown to become a global corporation.

Ericsson of today is an international leader in telecommunications, with some 55,000 employees in over 140 countries. Approximately 40 % of all mobile calls are made through Ericsson systems.

One of their latest products is the T600 mobile phone, which weighs only 60 grams with its lightweight battery and sleek design.

Tetra Pak Packaging

optimal and minimal solutions

"A package should save more than it costs" was the motto of Tetra Pak's founder Ruben Rausing (1895–1983), who developed the tetrahedron-shaped carton.

The basic idea was to shape a tube from a roll of plastic-coated paper, fill it with beverage and seal it from the underside. Thereby the nutritional value and the taste of the contents were preserved. The package itself was also easy to distribute and handle.

It all began in 1929, when Rausing and Erik Åkerlund established the first specialized packaging factory in Scandinavia. The company was called Åkerlund & Rausing and soon became one of the largest packaging manufacturers in Europe.

In 1951 AB Tetra Pak was founded, as a subsidiary in Lund, under the leadership of Rausing and Erik Wallenberg. On May 18, 1951, the new packaging system was introduced to the press, and received extensive coverage.

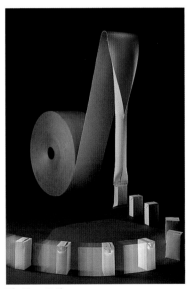

The first delivery of a Tetra Pak machine was in September 1951, to the Dairy Association of Lund. Even today, two thirds of products in Tetra Pak's packages are dairy products.

The company became part of the Tetra Laval Group in 1993, following a merger between Tetra Pak and the company Alfa-Laval. Net sales amounted to 7.5 billion euros in 2002.

The Tetra Brik system.

Anders Celsius

creator of our temperature scale

What made Anders Celsius (1701–1744) famous to future generations was his temperature scale, which he defined by choosing a 100 degree scale with the boiling and freezing points of water as fixed points.

Celsius was born into an academic family and later taught mathematics and astronomy at the University of Uppsala. He participated in an

expedition by the Paris Academy of Sciences in 1736 to measure the shape of the planet earth by measuring the length of a degree of the meridian (longitude). The result was that the earth proved to be a prolate sphere, bulging at its centre.

Anders Celsius carried out many geographical latitude measurements for the Swedish General Map, and was also probably the first to discover that the landmass of the Nordic countries has been slowly rising above sea level since the ice age.

In astronomy Celsius made observations of eclipses and various astronomical phenomena. He published tables of carefully determined magnitudes for a total of 300 stars, using his own photometric system. His technique consisted of using identical transparent glassplates through which he observed the star. The number of plates needed to obliterate the light from each star determined the magnitude of the star.

Celsius died in 1744, only 42 years old. Among his papers was found a draft of a science fiction novel with the plot situated partly on the star Sirius.

The Celsius temperature scale. Amongst other works he left behind was a book called Arithmetic for Swedish Youth, which was considered a unique publication for its time.

Spanners and Pliers

one size fits all

At the end of the 19th century all tools, screws, nuts and bolts were made by hand and no standardized sizes existed. The result was that for every nut and bolt, a suitable spanner had to be used. Most workers thought this was a very tiresome business. J.P. Johansson in Enköping was the first to do something about it!

In 1892 he came up with the ingenious idea of the adjustable spanner, which replaced several tools he had to carry before. Four years earlier he had invented the pipe wrench.

J.P. eventually met the entrepreneur B.A. Hjort, who had opened a tool and machinery company in Stockholm in 1889. With Hjort's business skills and Johansson's inventions, the road was open to success. The company B.A. Hjort & Co was thus founded, later abbreviated to BAHCO.

An adjustable spanner.

Today, BAHCO is part of the Sandvik Group and develops, manufactures and markets its hand tools and machines all over the world. The main office of the company is still situated in the small town of Enköping. Sandvik produces a continuous flow of new products, but it still leads the adjustable spanner market, which is now into its 6th generation.

Gustaf Dalén

Sweden's blind Edison

Gustaf Dalén joined the newly formed AGA company in 1904. With a succession of technically advanced solutions, he succeeded in revolutionising lighthouse technology, developing a technique to use acetylene gas in a safe, efficient and economical way.

In 1909 Gustaf Dalén became the Managing Director of AGA. He also took an active part in trials to develop a safe porous core for acetylene cylinders. In one such trial Dalén was seriously injured and permanently blinded. He was awarded the Nobel Prize in Physics in 1909 for his inventions connected with lighthouse technology.

Gustaf Dalén continued to energetically lead AGA until his death in

Gustaf Dalén received the Nobel Prize in Physics in 1909.

1937. Although blind, he designed the unique AGA cooker, which is still manufactured in England.

Since the beginning of the 1970's, AGA has gone through a massive restructuring, to be able to focus more on gases. Today, AGA – as part of the German Linde Group – produces and supplies gases and services to industrial, medical and speciality gas markets in some 40 countries.

AGA still follows Gustaf Dalén's motto: "Solve the customers' problems. Give them the opportunity to increase their profits, safety and quality in their operations. Help them to introduce new, improved technology."

The Three-Phase System

spreading light in the world

Jonas Wenström (1855–1893) was the son of an engineer and grew up in an industrial environment. After his technical studies Wenström travelled throughout Europe and the United States to visit technical exhibitions and also worked on various inventions. Wenström – contemporary with Thomas Alva Edison – contributed to the enormous industrial boom in Sweden at that time.

His most important invention was the three-phase electrical system, which also became the base for the development of the company ASEA (now ABB). In July 1891, he was granted the Swedish patent. The three-phase electrical system made it possible to use alternating electrical currents for industrial purposes,

Wenström made electrification profitable.

and made electrification profitable. Large areas could be provided with electricity from a central source. Power systems operating at different voltages could be interconnected; electricity could be transmitted over great distances and smoothly transformed to a suitable voltage level.

In the early days power stations consisted mainly of steam turbines and internal-combustion engines connected to dynamos, but they were soon replaced by hydraulic turbines connected to generators as the power transmission networks were enlarged.

Carl von Linné

the prince of botanists

Carl von Linné (1707–1778), born Linnaeus, is mainly famous for his systematic classification of plants, animals and minerals, which was presented in the publication Systema Naturae. Linnaeus made scientific research journeys in Sweden, which resulted in lengthy and detailed reports. More specifically, he travelled to the province of Lapland in 1732, to Dalarna in 1734 and finally to Skåne in 1749.

The Linné Garden is a dazzling oasis in the centre of Uppsala.

Linnaeus also sent colleagues to all corners of the world to collect specimens and report their observations: Anders Sparrman and Carl Peter Thunberg travelled to China; Sparrman and David Solander participated in James Cook's round-the-world expedition; Thunberg visited Japan; Johan Peter Falck explored the interior of Asia; Pehr Kalm travelled to North America, Anton Martin to the Artic Ocean, Daniel Rolander and Pehr Löfling to South America, Fredrik Hasselqvist to Palestine and Peter Forsskål to Arabia.

Only in recent years has it been possible to fully appreciate Linnaeus' eminence as a scientist, physician and especially as a botanist. His book Systema Naturae has been ranked one of the 100 books that have contributed most to the development of humanity. His insistence on empirical evidence for all conclusions furthered the cause of the inductive method in the natural sciences.

Volvo

innovative safety

The Volvo Car Corporation reported sales of about 400,000 car vehicles in 2002 and it employs 28,000 people. Since 1999, Ford Motor Company has wholly owned Volvo Car, but headquarters and vital components production mainly still reside in Sweden.

Volvo also produces a large range of products in the fields of transportation equipment and aerospace. For example, they develop and produce components for aircraft and rocket engines with high technology content, in cooperation with the world's leading aerospace companies.

Innovation plays an important role in the company – I-shift automatic transmission is one of the latest, important innovations for trucks. The name may be interpreted in two ways: in the literal meaning of "I shift" or as "Intelligent shift".

Volvo has also introduced the SIPS-system, together with the SIPS-bag, which reduces the risk of severe injury from side-impact by 40 %.

PHOTO: VOLVO

Volvo – quality and safety.

Saab

in space and on land

Saab – Svenska Aeroplan Aktiebolaget – was founded in 1937 as a national manufacturer of military aircraft.

Cutting edge aircrafts.

Innovative car design.

Today, the Group consists of two primary divisions: the automobile division (partly owned by General Motors) and the division focusing on defence, aviation and space.

Saab is active in more than 50 countries worldwide. A forerunner when it comes to car technology, Saab was the first car manufacturer to introduce seat belts as standard and also to develop a turbo engine for everyday use.

For over 60 years Saab has also developed high-technology defence and non-defence systems. Saab's defence/aviation operations are organized in six business areas, covering modern information defence technologies, command and control systems, military and commercial aircraft, advanced technical support and services, missiles, space equipment and aviation services.

Hennes & Mauritz

global fashion concept

The clothing chain HM – Hennes & Mauritz – was founded in 1947 and has expanded into owning over 900 stores in over 18 countries, and during 2003 over a hundred new stores were planned. Since HM works with many different concepts, the store size can vary between 300 and 3,000 square metres!

Over half a billion articles are sold each year and the company employs almost 40,000 co-workers.

HM's business idea, much like IKEA's, is to offer fashion and quality at the best prices. In addition to the stores, the company also runs a mail order business called Rowells, and in some Nordic countries sales are performed over the Internet. HM also markets cosmetic products under their own label.

Some fashion trends are anticipated up to one year in advance, both when it comes to colour and different models. The hottest and most recent fashion is caught with much less notice, down to two weeks – from the streets, exhibitions, movies and magazines.

Absolut

success in a bottle

About forty million litres of Absolut Vodka is shipped and consumed in one year and every drop of it comes from the distilleries near Åhus in southern Sweden, a small town of barely 10,000 inhabitants.

With the 100th anniversary of "Absolutely Pure Vodka" closing in, the company made the decision to export a new vodka. Modern distilling techniques would be used, creating a new product that was a century old: Absolut Vodka.

The famous bottle of Absolut Vodka.

Myron Poloner, a co-worker at the advertising company used, fell in love with the bottle. And one night it struck him. The bottle should have no label at all! You should be able to see right through it. The vodka should be an elegant vodka for well-educated, wealthy people, who liked to show off a little bit at parties...

In 1980, the New York Times published the first Absolut Vodka ad in the form in which it has remained to date. Absolut and the TBWA advertising agency began a dazzling and very long advertising campaign. Over 1,400 ads have been created to this date, and are a tribute to the imagination and creativity of really good advertising.

Hasselblad

a capturing company

The company Hasselblad & Co. was founded already in 1841. When Arvid Viktor Hasselblad, son of the company's founder and an enthusiastic amateur photographer, established a photographic division within the company, he is reported to have said: "I certainly don't think that we will earn much money on this, but at least it will allow us to take pictures for free."

Today, Hasselblad is a global camera equipment corporation owned by Shriro with the reputation of making the world's finest cameras.

Their cameras have even been used in space and the company has a long collaboration record with NASA. When man landed on the moon for the first time, Hasselblad's equipment was used. The list of breathtaking images is almost endless. A single man hovering in space, the earth as seen from the moon, the first step...

A close cooperation is also maintained with the Erna and Victor Hasselblad Foundation, an independent, non-profit organization founded in 1979. The Foundation's primary purpose is to promote research and academic teaching in the natural sciences and photography.

PHOTO: HASSELBLAD

The choice of many professional photographers.

Dynamite Stuff

in safe packages

The great inventor Alfred Nobel was a truly international man. He was born in Stockholm in 1833, received an international education in St. Petersburg from 1842, and travelled extensively. After returning to Sweden in 1863 he became a chemist at his father's laboratory in Stockholm.

During his life Nobel held 355 patents, of which his most important was dynamite. He also perfected the explosive nitroglycerine, using a method developed by the Italian scientist Sobrero. In 1864, a huge explosion in Nobel's factory killed his youngest brother Emil. He then decided to make explosives safer and found his answer in dynamite, which was patented in 1866. Other inventions included the detonating cap, synthetic rubber and synthetic leather. In 1888 he received another patent for ballistite, the first smokeless powder.

Dynamite was patented in 1866.

Alfred Nobel's fortune was founded on his great inventions. Around these he had established companies in about ninety locations in twenty countries. Alfred Nobel's greatness "lay in the ability to combine the penetrating mind of the scientist and inventor with the forward-looking dynamism of the industrialist".

Many of the companies founded by Nobel have developed into industrial enterprises that still play an important role in the world economy, for example Imperial Chemical Industries, Great Britain; Société Centrale de Dynamite, France and Dyno Industries in Norway. Toward the end of his life, Nobel acquired the company AB Bofors in Karlskoga, where Björkborn Manor became his home. Alfred Nobel passed away in San Remo on December 10, 1896.

Alfa Laval

a man with an idea

A man with an idea – that was the beginning of the worldwide Alfa Laval Group. The man was Gustaf de Laval and his invention was the first "continuously operating cream separator". The year was 1877.

Based on this invention, the company AB Separator was formed and soon grew into an international enterprise and the world's leading separator manufacturer.

Throughout the years to come technical innovation set the character of the company. The Alfa patent from 1889 was one of the key technical innovations. Henceforth, the separators were called Alfa Laval, which in 1963 also was to become the name of the company.

The prototype of the first separator from 1878.

The separator principle has other applications than milk separation. As early as 1898, a yeast separator was introduced. Shortages of lubricating oil during World War I led to the development of a separator for oil purification. Already, in these formative years, the industrial separator had secured a foothold.

Separators dominated Alfa Laval's production for many years, but in the 1930's heat exchangers became an important part of the product range. Other competence areas were added later, forming Alfa Laval today with its special skills of Separation, Heat Transfer, Flow Technology and Automation. The company combines these key competences in solutions for customers within a broad range of fields including the process industry, shipping, waste water treatment and power generation.

The Alfa Laval Group, which is part of Tetra Laval, has 13,500 employees and 110 subsidiaries in 50 countries.

Dr Engström's Respirator

improving the survival odds

In the early 1950's a polio epidemic struck the Nordic countries and many victims were treated with primitive mechanical ventilation of the airways – "iron lungs". Unfortunately, the patients' condition declined rapidly and the mortality rate was very high.

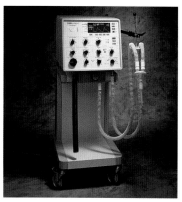

The respirator.

A Swedish physician, Dr Carl-Gunnar Engström, had previously analysed the blood gases of polio victims. He concluded that the crude iron lung was ineffective. Racing against time, he and his team developed a more effective machine. Unlike its predecessor, the new Engström ventilator effectively insufflated air or oxygen directly into the patient's respiratory system. The new ventilator was introduced in 1951, reducing mortality among polio victims and other patients in intensive care. Shortly afterwards, the first anaesthesia ventilator was introduced, based on the same principle. In the following few years, Dr Engström's invention dramatically improved the survival odds in the world's intensive care units.

The clinical concept remains the same to this day, although continued research and clinical experience have resulted in increasingly sophisticated technical solutions. These include the world's first electronic, fully integrated anaesthesia system in 1988. Today, information technology and system integration are the core of evolution in intensive care.

The Safety Match

an enlightening invention

At the beginning of the 19th century many countries were experimenting with different ways of lighting fire, primarily with matches, which contained poisonous white phosphorus. The Swedish chemistry professor Gustaf Erik Pasch (1788–1862) developed the safety match in 1844. He separated out the phosphorus and turned it into a less poisonous and less flammable form (red phosphorus), which he put on to a separate striking surface.

Swedish Safety Match.

Pasch patented his solution and in 1844 the first matches were produced. Success was not immediate as the matches were too expensive. The factory was closed and the patent expired.

Johan Edvard and Carl Frans Lundström opened a match factory in 1845 and improved Pasch's invention. They renewed the patent and introduced it at the 1855 World Exhibition in Paris. The safety match was awarded the silver medal and received much attention.

The real breakthrough came when the mechanic Alexander Lagerman was hired in 1870. He had constructed the first automatic match machine already in 1864 and had improved it ever since. The safety match was finally mass-produced with high quality and low price!

Since 1987 Swedish Match in Tidaholm has been Sweden's sole match factory. They, among other things, produce the Solstickan matches, and a portion of the revenue from all products in the Solstickan family goes to a foundation that assists children and the elderly.

The Incredible Zip Device

symbol of modern life

If you look in Grolier's American encyclopaedia, it says that the zip was invented by Whitcomb Jones in 1893, who had a patent on an automatic device which opened and closed a shoe. However, in reality the invention did not work.

When the zip "Ccurity" made its entrance onto the market, it often broke, became rusty and even had to be removed before washing the clothes. From this idea Swedish electronics engineer Gideon Sundbäck tried in vain to improve the Ccurity zip and eventually realized that he had to find a device without its hooks and eyes.

The zip has made life much easier.

After a few months of intense work he came up with a solution which worked. In December 1913 Gideon's zip was ready. Looking much the same as today, his zip could be bent without opening and did not rust. Still, it would take another 20 years before the zip was mass-produced.

By 1930, 100 million zips were sold in the United States. Its unique features had finally been recognized and the zip became a symbol of modern life. What happened to Gideon Sundbäck? He devoted the rest of his life to improving the zip and its manufacturing techniques. At the beginning of the 1940's he retired to Ohio as a wealthy man and died in 1954.

Epoch-making Medicine

Losec cures ulcers

Astra's (now AstraZeneca) revolutionary ulcer medicine Losec was approved as a medicine in 1988 after more than twenty years of research and development. The project started in 1966 at Hässle, and the goal was to find something, which would effectively restrict the hydrochloric acid production in the stomach, thereby creating a remedy for one of the main causes of ulcers.

In 1973 the pharmacologist Sven Erik Sjöstrand and the chemist Ulf Ljunggren succeeded in producing and clinically testing the first bensimidazol compound – the chemical basic structure for Losec. The chemist Arne Brändström has further developed the drug.

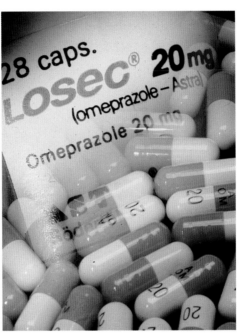

Losec restricts acid in the stomach.

Losec's function was unknown in detail until the end of the 1970's, when it was shown that the bensimidazoles block the proton pump, an enzyme compound, which regulates the acid production in the stomach.

IKEA

form & function for the masses

Ingvar Kamprad was born in southern Sweden in 1926, and started his professional life as a young lad who sold matches to his neighbours. When he was 17, he used a money gift to found his own business, IKEA (notice how the first two initials are made up of his name). After a while, he began advertising in local papers and started a mail order business. Soon, furniture made by locals became part of his product range. In 1951, they became the exclusive focus of IKEA. The company, as we know it today, had been born!

IKEA's vision is based on the idea of improved every day life – through offering a wide range of products, with good form and function at the best possible price, so that as many as possible can afford to buy them.

The main reason why IKEA began designing its own products pretty soon, was that competitors pressured the suppliers and some of them boycotted IKEA. So they had no choice but to design their own furniture. And then on top of it, a co-worker had a bright idea – why not transport the furniture in flat packages? Less damage, less work and less space.

A pattern was forming that became the IKEA way: to turn a problem into an opportunity.

In 2002, the company's turnover amounted to 11 billion Euro and over 70,000 people work within the foundation.

Popular Profiles

Athletes

Björn Borg

Brilliant tennis player with fantastic baseline play and an athletic ability that often enabled him to retrieve seemingly impossible shots. Borg won the Wimbledon five years in a row, 1976–80.

Ingemar Stenmark

Alpine skier from northern Sweden, with three World Cup championships, 86 World Cup wins in sixteen years and two gold medals at the 1980 Olympics.

Sven-Göran Eriksson

The Swedish trainer who was brought in to "save" English football after a defeat to Germany. Declared a hero after he took the English team to the 2002 World Cup Finals.

Annika Sörenstam

This brilliant Swedish golf pro is considered the women's Tiger Woods, with more than 40 career LPGA victories.

Musicians

Roxette

Pop duo with Per Gessle and Marie Fredriksson. Their second album Look Sharp (1988) sold 8 million copies. Roxette has hit the US first spot three times.

Ace of Base

Pop group with the siblings Jonas, Malin and Jenny Berggren, plus Ulf Ekberg. Their megahits, such as Happy Nation and All That She Wants, have been played in over 40 countries.

ABBA

World famous ABBA produced nine No. 1 singles and eight chart-topping albums in the UK and their success in the US was also spectacular. Their biggest hit was "Dancing Queen" in 1976.

Max Martin

Brilliant hit maker, who worked with celebrities such as Britney Spears and Backstreet Boys.

Birgit Nilsson

Famous female opera singer who has sung all over the world – Beirut, Vienna, London, New York... Her voice is a soprano of extraordinary volume and she has few equals in the world.

Writers

Selma Lagerlöf (1858–1940)

Celebrated writer who broke through with the novel Gösta Berlings Saga in 1897. She is most well known for Nils Holgersson's Wonderful Adventures and for winning the Nobel Prize in 1909.

August Strindberg (1849–1912)

Contemporary to Ibsen, Strindberg is mostly known internationally through his dramas – for example the Father and Miss Julie. His love and marriage plays were seen as very radical at the time.

Vilhelm Moberg (1898–1973)

Very productive author, famous for the four novels in the epic The Emigrants. Moberg focused on the agrarian and proletarian Sweden and the injustices at the time.

Astrid Lindgren (1907-2002)

Voted as Swede of the Century, she has written 88 children's books, which have been translated into 85 languages, and sold in 120 million copies. One of her most well-known characters is Pippi Longstocking.

Actors

Greta Garbo (1905–1990)

This mysterious beauty went to Hollywood in 1924. In 1954 she won an Oscar for "her unforgettable screen performances". She retired already in 1941, leading a guarded personal life.

Ingrid Bergman (1915–1982)

Called "Sweden's illustrious gift to Hollywood", she made several films that established her as a class actress: Casablanca, Gaslight, Anastasia... The two last, she won Oscars for.

Pernilla August

Seen as the latest heir to the tradition of radiant actresses, she has been associated with Bergman's movies. To the American public she is most known as Shmi – the mother of Darth Vader in Star Wars.

Max von Sydow

Recognized as Sweden's foremost contemporary film star. Has a long and successful career with unforgettable movies such as Bergman's the Seventh Seal and the blockbuster the Exorcist.

Directors

Ingmar Bergman

A colossus among movie and theatre directors, he has earned universal reverence through his penetrating vision. Among his most famous movies are the Seventh Seal and Fanny & Alexander.

Lasse Hallström

Hallström gained an international audience with My Life as A Dog in 1985. The movie earned him two Oscar nominations. He has also directed Chocolate and the Cider House Rules. Married to Swedish actress Lena Olin.

Painters

Anders Zorn (1860–1920)

Well-known painter and sculptor, remembered mainly for his exquisite realistic nudes. At the 1900 Paris Universal Exhibition he was awarded the French Legion of Honour.

Carl Larsson (1853–1919)

Deeply loved artist who captured contemporary home life and culture with his children as his favourite models. He and his wife, Karin, furnished a very special house, which can be visited in Sundborn, Dalarna.

Political profiles

Dag Hammarskjöld (1905–1961)

Secretary-General of the United Nations in 1953 and re-elected in 57. A brilliant mind, he introduced new procedures into the UN, such as the presence of UN in troubled spots. His plane crashed tragically in 1961.

Raoul Wallenberg (1912–?)

Wallenberg helped about 100,000 Hungarian Jews escape Nazi executions. He was later reportedly arrested in Moscow, never to be heard of again.

Swedish Traditions

A country's traditions and celebrations are often the most interesting aspects of a culture. In the following pages you will learn how Swedes celebrate the important holidays of Christmas and Easter.

You will also be introduced to festivities you have probably never heard of, such as the Crayfish Party and Walpurgis Eve.

Events of Easter

resurrection in religion and nature

Swedish Easter celebrations are not only a tribute to the death and resurrection of Christ, but also a celebration of the "rebirth" of spring. This is a moveable feast (March–April) and Swedish workers get four days holiday – Friday to Monday.

Witches are seen at Easter. Old superstition claims that these witches would fly to the devil's lodgings, the Blue Mountain, on Thursday before Easter to plot their evil doings. Today, if you see a witch in Sweden during Easter, she will probably not frighten you. Little girls, with painted faces, dress up in head scarves and long skirts and go from house to house to collect sweets in a coffee pot.

Birch twigs decorated with colourful feathers can be bought in almost every market place during Lent and are symbols of spring and the torment of Christ.

What would Easter be in most Christian countries without eggs? The egg is basically an old religious symbol for resurrection and it is also associated with this particular season. The art of painting eggs is also practised in Sweden and almost all homes are decorated with a bowl filled with multicoloured eggs. Children also receive Easter eggs filled with sweets, which are supposed to be a gift from the Easter rabbit.

Good Friday begins the Easter celebrations. It is a day of sorrow and represents the day when Christ died on the cross. In the past, people would remain at home, dress in mourning clothes and go to church, where they would spend most of the day.

On this sad day, in olden times, people were not allowed to eat meat because of Lent, and ate only fish. Swedes served only salted herring and drank no water, to remind themselves of Christ's suffering.

The day after Good Friday, Easter Eve, would mean the end of solemn times. Once again one could eat, rejoice and clean the house! This would also be the day when the bonfires and firecrackers would be lit, as the witches were supposed to return from the Blue Mountain. In general, people prepared for the big celebration. Today many Swedish families gather round the Easter dinner table to celebrate in a setting of daffodils, coloured eggs and delicious food.

On the day of joy and resurrection – Easter Day – the paschal lamb is prepared. In Sweden this is a novel custom and derives from the Passover celebrated by the Israelites in Egypt, according to the Bible. The lamb also symbolises Christ himself, who was sacrificed for man's sake.

PHOTO: CD BILDARKIV

Three little Easter witches.

Walpurgis Eve and Mayday

the wooing of spring

On the doorstep to Spring, on the last day of April, Swedes celebrate Walpurgis Eve with choral singing, speeches and, most importantly, crackling bonfires. According to ancient tradition, the bonfires were lit to scare off the wild animals from the pastures where the cattle would graze from the first day of May. Some say that this celebration is in honour of Saint Valborg (Walpurgis).

The bonfires are the central theme of these festivities, and they are lit on high places where they can be seen from a great distance.

The following day Swedes celebrate the national Mayday holiday. In olden times it was a secular festival, or a kind of "peoples party" combined with a court and the merchant assembly. This tradition developed and, in the 1880's, the labour movement selected this day for its annual celebration and parades. As time went by, this event grew larger and today includes workers' rallies, debates, speeches and other activities associated with labour and human rights issues in general. Flags, banners and brass bands are the most common features of this day!

PHOTO: ANDERS DAMBERG

The Walpurgis bonfire lights up the darkness.

Swedes dance schottis and polka around the Midsummer pole.

Midsummer Merrymaking

ringdances, games and music

In June the days grow longer and the evenings lighter and, on Midsummer Eve, light has finally won over darkness – the day more or less never ends. Originally, Midsummer was the holiday of John the Baptist, but it has become more of a celebration to the glory of summer and to light. Midsummer is celebrated on the weekend closest to the actual Midsummer Day, June 24, when the ancient summer solstice festival was probably once held.

On an open field of grass, a tall pole is laid out for people to decorate with leaves and flowers. Sometimes ribbons and other paper decorations are also tied around the pole and from a crossbar two circles with flowers are hung. Later on, all the guests arrive, many in traditional dress. With the help of the fiddler and the accordionist's music, the men push up the midsummer pole against the sky. The celebrations begin!

People join hands and dance around the pole to traditional tunes, and the children play many games.

After these ceremonies, people go home and enjoy the Midsummer meal, consisting of herring and new potatoes served with sour cream and chopped chives. This was actually the poor man's dish in olden times; herring was eaten almost every day together with potatoes, and served with soured milk. The mix of salt, sour, strong and sweet tastes makes it a very interesting culinary experience.

Beer and schnapps will be served as well, and tasty strawberries for dessert are a must. The table itself is often decorated with a Swedish flag and a lovely bouquet of daisies, poppies and cornflowers, which are typical Midsummer flowers picked in the fields.

There is also a lot of magic going on at Midsummer. For those girls interested in finding out whom their husband to-be is, there is a special trick. If you secretly go out into the fields and pick seven different kinds of flowers and put them under your pillow, you will dream of your future love.

At one time Swedes danced around a bonfire, but it failed to create the right effect because of the lightness of the night! As a result, the Swedes imported the Maypole from Germany and turned it into a Midsummer pole to dance around.

Crayfish under the Moon

a messy but tasty business

As a last goodbye to summer, the Crayfish Party has become one of the most typical of Swedish traditions. On the first Thursday in August, "crayfish hysteria" breaks out in Sweden; people go on shopping sprees to buy Chinese lanterns, funny hats, huge paper bibs and napkins decorated with crayfish motifs. The table is laid out for the party and on mild late summer evenings the garden chairs are taken out, the lanterns are hung up and Swedes wrap themselves in blankets, eating crayfish until well after dusk has fallen.

This unusual custom can be traced back to the Swedish authorities, who, a century ago, permitted crayfish only to be caught for two months a year, starting in August, to save their becoming extinct. What is rare often becomes precious, and this was the case for the Swedish crayfish. Consequently, it was a cause for celebration when the Swedes could finally again enjoy these black gems of the water. Most of the crayfish served today at these parties are not of Swedish origin. Turkish, Spanish and American crayfish have replaced them, as a crayfish plague almost annihilated the Swedish species in 1907.

Crayfish used to be caught with bag nets at night, but today people put out crayfish cages in the evening and empty them in the morning with great anticipation.

There are as many different ways of boiling crayfish as there are cooks.

Basically, the newly caught crayfish are rinsed and then boiled in a special bouillon and then soaked in fresh water flavoured with dill. The cooked crayfish remain in the water until they are cold and have acquired the delicious taste of dill and salt.

The golden red crayfish are arranged on large dishes decorated with fresh dill crowns. According to tradition, toast or crisp bread with butter is prepared, and some well-ripened strong cheese may also be served.

Traditionally, beer and schnapps are served with the crayfish. Every now and then a "drinking song" is sung and then a toast is proposed: "Skål"! The schnapps keeps you warm in the chilly late summer night and at the same time refreshes your taste buds before enjoying the next delicacy.

Early Autumn Delicacies

different culinary experiences

Two fish dishes, the herring and the eel, have given rise to two Autumn festivals in Sweden, one in the north and one in the south. Even though these culinary feasts are celebrated in different corners of this oblong country, they have the same theme, namely food!

Fermented Baltic herring, "surströmming", is actually a hangover from the times people could afford only as much salt as to allow the fish to ferment instead of rot.

Today the fermented herring is produced and canned commercially on some islands in the Gulf of Bothnia, and the extended fermentation makes the tin bulge. When opened, the smell is dreadful, so many northern Swedes open the tin under water to avoid the explosive smell!

This ritual dish, which has become so dear to the northern inhabitants, is served with the northern Swedish potato, which is yellow and almond-shaped. The fish and the potatoes are rolled in a thin bread slice with onions and butter. Everything is literally washed down with beer, schnapps or even milk. Those who have managed to eat three or four herrings can be proud, it is quite an achievement. For dessert cloudberries can be enjoyed. This golden berry grows in the northern swamplands, and with its fresh taste, it is an expensive delicacy.

For our southern friends, the eel is a symbol of the coming Autumn. The expression "eel darkness", refers to darker autumn nights and alludes to the fact that the eels, because of the lack of light, can no longer see the nets.

At an eel party, eel is exactly what you will see and eat; boiled, smoked, fried, grilled and even stuffed, all in all there are ten to twelve different ways of preparing the eel. This fish dish is also helped along with one or two glasses of schnapps, since it is hard for many stomachs to digest.

At some eel parties and restaurants an "eel king" is crowned with a paper crown for catching the highest number of live eels from a barrel with his bare hands!

During the Thirty Years' War fermented herring was delivered to Swedish soldiers by boat to different war zones around Europe.

55

St. Martin's Goose Eve

a feast devoted to food

On St. Martin's Goose Eve, on November 10, people from the southern province of Skåne gather at home or in restaurants for the annual goose menu and to enjoy a welcome break from everyday life. It is still a while until Christmas and the landscape is veiled in a grey and rainy atmosphere.

Geese are the focus of this celebration because this fine-tasting bird has always been a symbol of Skåne, just as the reindeer is of Lapland. The reason why this celebration exists mainly in Skåne today is because geese are more abundant there, thanks to the many grazing pastures.

Selma Lagerlöf's book about Nils Holgersson, who rode on a goose from Skåne all the way to northern Sweden, has made the Swedish geese famous to children outside the country!

As a first course for the celebration meal the much disputed black soup (made of goose blood) will be served, called by some a delicacy and by others too much of an acquired taste. It looks a bit like chocolate pudding and is often decorated with slices of prunes and apples. After the soup the roasted goose will be served, crispy and juicy, with boiled potatoes and gravy to go with it. As a traditional dessert an impressive meringue tower called "spettekaka" will be eaten, which consists of a mixture of copious quantities of eggs and sugar which is dripped onto a spit. This cake used to be eaten all over Sweden, but today it is considered a speciality of Skåne.

In olden times the eating of goose on St. Martin's Eve was reserved for the wealthy and later for rich farmers. Often marriages were combined with this celebration and great festivities were arranged. The dinner could include soup, dried ling, rice porridge, goose steak, pork steaks and cheese cake. According to an old manuscript from Lund, the guests at a wedding once gave 24 geese to a bridal couple! Originally, the celebration of Mårten (Martin) was in honour of the French Martin of Tours, and was also connected to the time for tasting the new vintage. Of course a good wine had to be accompanied by a good meal – fat geese were abundant at that time of year – and thus the connection Martin–wine–goose was created.

The Lucia parade enlightens the darkness of December.

Lucia, Lusse Cats and Starboys

celebration of light heralding Christmas

One of the Swedish traditions which seems most exotic to a foreign visitor is the Lucia celebration on December 13. Hotel guests are often woken up early in the morning by a gentle knock on the door and are faced with something resembling an apparition; a girl with a crown of white candles wearing a white robe with a red ribbon around her waist is singing with her hands pressed together like a saint.

Behind her follow girls in white robes holding candles and with tinsel in their hair. Last in the procession are the Starboys ("stjärngossar"), holding paper stars on a stick and wearing conical hats decorated with stars, symbolizing the star of Bethlehem. After singing a few Lucia carols, these angels of light will offer their audience saffron-flavoured buns called "Lusse Cats" and then be off to surprise the next guest.

Exactly how Lucia came to Sweden from Syracuse, Italy, where she was the patron saint, no one really knows. It seems as though several legends and traditions have merged to become the Lucia celebrations we know today. One origin seems to have been the very old midwinter solstice festival around the time of Lucia. Lucia, which means light, became the symbol of someone who would entice the sun in times of darkness. Until quite recently the celebration of Lucia was local to western Sweden only, but during the last century it spread to the entire country. Today Swedes can see Lucia at home, at work, in school and in a public parade in each town.

At home the children often enact Lucia. In their costumes they prepare coffee and Lusse Cats and begin their parade. The parents are supposed to be sleeping and are woken by the flickering candles and the sound of Lucia songs. Afterwards everyone sinks their teeth into the yellow buns and maybe some gingersnaps! Sometimes children also go from house to house singing in the hope of being offered a gift of sweets or a coin, something especially appreciated by the elderly. The public procession is most often preceded by a competition in the local papers for the most suitable Lucia – preferably a girl with long blond hair. The parade is held after dark through town, and often the Lucia travels in a wagon with torches, followed by the other girls, star boys and a couple of "elves".

The Tale of Christmas

a candle is lit to dispel the darkness

When the first of four Advent Candles is lit in Swedish homes and churches, there are three more weeks until the arrival of Christmas on December 24. Candles and the concept of light are very central to the Swedish Christmas celebration, because the festival falls when "it is not day, it is not night, it balances between the two".

Originally, pagan Swedes celebrated something called the Midwinter feast around the time of present day Christmas, wanting to bring out the sun again through sacrifices and drinking to the memory of the gods. As Christianity made its way into Sweden, the feast became a celebration of the birth of Jesus Christ – the bearer of light – and the original pagan traditions became entwined with Christian customs.

Christmas – "Jul" (Yule) in Swedish – is the most important holiday in Sweden and is preceded by many preparations. The Christmas tree must be collected and decorated, the food cooked and the Christmas gifts wrapped.

The Christmas tree is a symbol of the burning bush in which God revealed himself to Moses, and is therefore decorated with burning candles or, today, usually electric lights. In Sweden the tree is most often a freshly cut spruce which is decorated with a variety of glass balls and ornaments a few days before Christmas Eve.

The Swedish Christmas table is loaded with delicacies and often attractively decorated, quite a sight for the foreign eye. This dinner is usually eaten on Christmas Eve, the most important day of Christmas in Sweden.

If you take a closer look at this splendid table, you will notice many pork dishes, which might seem peculiar to the uninitiated. Normally pigs were slaughtered in autumn, and only one or two were saved for Christmas. From the autumn to Christmas, the Swedes had had to settle for cured meat and were, of course, thrilled to eat fresh meat at Christmas. In olden days, the meal was preceded by slaughtering, baking, brewing, candle making and cleaning, and this abundance would ensure a good new year.

The Christmas Eve meal begins with the "smörgåsbord", a mix of pickled fishes and other small dishes such as fried meatballs, eel and liver pâté. The main dish of the meal is lightly salted ham, which is first boiled, then covered with beaten egg and breadcrumbs and finally roasted. Christmas Eve is actually often referred to as the "dipping day", which alludes to the fact that people were allowed to dip their bread into the broth from the ham.

PHOTO: KNUT E. SVENSSON/IMS

The delicious Swedish Christmas table.

Some households also eat dried ling, which has been soaked in lye and water. This is a dish that stems from the times when fresh fish was hard to get, but fish was still necessary to eat after the long Christmas fast for repentance.

No Swedish Christmas table would be complete without rice pudding, which is eaten as a dessert. Several games are associated with the pudding; an almond is hidden in it, and whoever gets it has to invent a rhyme, often alluding to some gift.

Christmas gifts are the highlight for the children. Much to their anguish, the presents are opened late, after the Christmas Eve meal. "Julklapp" is the Swedish word for Christmas gift and literally means Christmas knock. According to folklore, people would knock on your door, throw the gift in and then run away. In the past the family members, especially children and servants, would receive bread, cheese and a candle.

"Jultomten" is the central Father Christmas figure in Swedish homes. He is the Swedish version of St. Nicholas, a saint known in many European countries for giving children his Christmas gifts. Swedes seem to have integrated the white-bearded St. Nicholas with the small elves which according to myth protected the farms. Custom says that one should put out some porridge for the elf to keep him in a good mood, and over time this fairy tale figure came into the house and handed out the gifts. Today, Jultomten arrives after dinner with a bag of gifts and also distributes the presents from under the Christmas tree. He is dressed in red and often exclaims "Are there any good children here?", which fills the children with fear and excitement at the same time!

Churchgoing has become less frequent in Sweden but many people still attend the early service on Christmas Day, which begins at seven o'clock in the morning when it is still pitch-black outside! In the past, people would arrive at church in torch-lit horse sleighs and be met by the sight of a church flooded with candlelight both outside and inside, reflected by the white snow.

At Christmas time the landscape frequently lies under a blanket of snow.

A Map
of Sweden

1. Skåne
2. Blekinge
3. Halland
4. Småland
5. Öland
6. Gotland
7. Bohuslän
8. Västergötland
9. Östergötland

10. Dalsland
11. Närke
12. Södermanland
13. Värmland
14. Västmanland
15. Uppland
16. Dalarna
17. Gästrikland
18. Hälsingland

19. Härjedalen
20. Medelpad
21. Jämtland
22. Ångermanland
23. Västerbotten
24. Lappland
25. Norrbotten

64

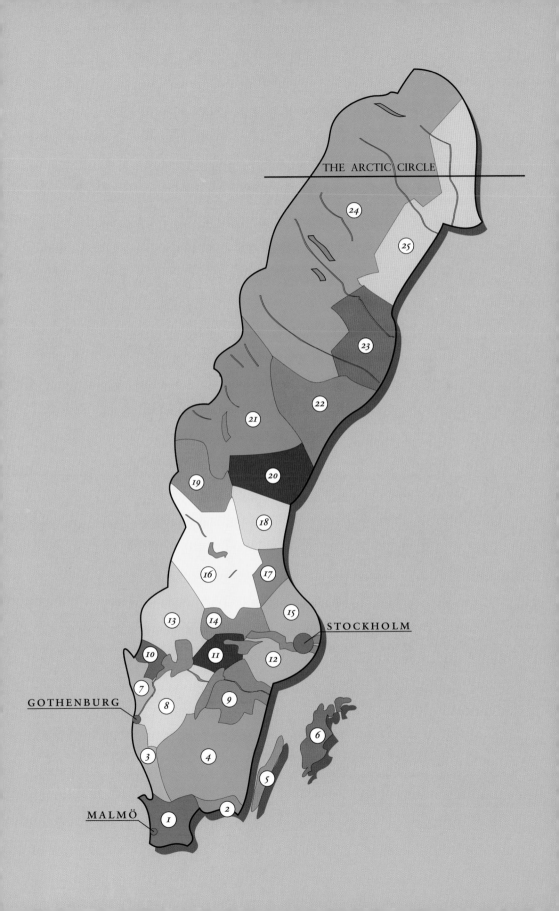

THE ARCTIC CIRCLE

STOCKHOLM

GOTHENBURG

MALMÖ

The Provinces of Sweden

This chapter reveals some of Sweden's most beautiful and interesting places – a scent of Sweden in other words. Under the headlines Southern, Central, Northern Sweden and Idyllic Islands you will find sites and natural areas worth visiting.

Southern Sweden

cultivated plains and sandy beaches

In the southernmost part of Sweden you can find everything your heart desires, from crowded cities and picturesque fishing villages to sandy beaches, forests and open sea. The landscape is sometimes described as flat, but actually it is an area with both undulating plains and steep hills.

This tip of the Scandinavian peninsula is the most densely populated area in Sweden. The traveller will notice that there is almost always a house within sight even in the countryside.

The province of Skåne resembles a huge garden, which is strikingly evident when the yellow rape flowers bloom in the fields against the blue summer sky. This part has also been called the granary of Sweden, since most agricultural activities are concentrated here because of the very fertile soil.

Situated in Skåne's southeastern corner is Österlen, a notable part of Southern Sweden. This 800 square kilometre area has an open landscape and a unique environment. Idyllic scenery and rolling hills leading to endless white beaches have made Österlen a popular place for both Swedes and

Glimmingehus is a mediaeval fortress built in 1499.

The mystical Ale's Stones from the Bronze Age.

67

foreigners. Many painters, writers and poets have found their inspiration from the rich culture of the region – Österlen has often been called the Provence of Sweden!

Southern Sweden has an abundance of ancient monuments; monoliths, burial mounds, rune stones and rock carvings from the Viking Era and the Bronze Age. One of the most significant sites is the mystical Ale's Stones outside Kåseberga. Situated on an impressive hill, surrounded by sea on three sides, and referred to as the Swedish "Stonehenge", it consists of huge blocks of stones set out in the outline of a ship. Scientists are still uncertain about its purpose, but some claim that it is a remnant of an astronomical construction from the Bronze Age.

Southern Sweden is also renowned for its many grand castles and manor houses. Österlen's Glimmingehus is a fortress built in 1499 by the Danish knight Ulfstand (Skåne was Danish at that time). This ancient castle can be seen for miles around with its stepped gable and orange-tiled roof.

Ulfstand commissioned a Westphalian architect to create the impregnable features of the building; slits instead of windows, thick sandstone walls and a wide moat. The building stands as a very vivid reminder of Österlen's medieval past.

The hills at Brösarp in southern Sweden are swathed in green in springtime.

Another site worth visiting is the 16th century Trollenäs Castle with its magnificent interior and renowned portrait gallery. It is often called "the dolls' castle" because of its exhibits of dolls with a folklore theme.

Prominent features of the landscape are the hundreds of white, lime-washed parish churches which stand among the fertile fields, some of them 800–900 years old. One of the most interesting is St. Olof's Church, north of Simrishamn. The beautiful sanctuary holds many priceless paintings and relics, including a wooden statue of Saint Olof. In his hand he holds a silver axe, which according to legend healed sick pilgrims. The axe has been touched innumerable times over the centuries and is an object of veneration for many visitors.

The small island of Ven outside Landskrona on the western coast is also characteristic of southern Sweden. Small boats from Landskrona or Råå take the visitor there, where the famous Backa slopes can be seen from the 13th century St. Ibb's Church. A large number of archaeological finds from all over the island show that the land has been used since the Stone Age. The world-famous astronomer Tycho Brahe lived there between 1575 and 1597, during which time he built the Uranienborg Manor in Dutch renaissance style and the Stjärneborg Observatory. The manor house was later demolished but the observatory has been restored. Brahe's careful observations, which were expanded by Kepler, led to the modern heliocentric conception of the Solar System.

The gastronomic traditions of the south are still cherished. The "smörgåsbord" – famous outside the Swedish borders – was originally a tradition from Skåne. A smörgåsbord is a large table filled with many delicacies. With this table, wealthy farmers could demonstrate their affluence on the farm. Traditionally, the dishes are eaten in the following order; first pickled herring in various styles, eel, salmon and other fish. Then the meat, including meatballs, goose, boiled ham and sliced beef. Finally, a selection of cheeses, fruit and tasty desserts, rounded off by the meringue "spettekaka". Eat as much as you want!

Central Sweden

the heart of the country

Småland is the province of never ending forests. Enormous amounts of wood are needed to fire the large furnaces when making glass out of sand. King Gustav Vasa brought a Venetian glass blower to Sweden and the industry was introduced. In 1556 the first glass was blown in the country and the first consignment was melted in Kosta, Småland, in the summer of 1742. The Kingdom of Glass was born!

The glassworks in Kosta is Sweden's oldest. Handmade glass is still made here. The surroundings have been very well kept through the centuries and are characterized by small red cottages with white corners. Kosta has often been called the mother glassworks of the Swedish glass industry. When the actual Kingdom of Glass was founded at the end of the 19th century, many of the glass blowers came from Kosta. Today, southern Småland is filled with fine glassworks, such as Orrefors, Kosta Boda, Sandvik and Johansfors. This emphasizes the spirit of Småland – craftmanship and quality.

Orrefors became pioneers of the world-famous Swedish glass, when they employed designers in 1915. With this decision the well-known Gate-Hald epoc began. Since then the glassworks have employed artists more and more, and today most of the works have their own designers and distinct styles. Visitors to Sweden should consider buying a piece of crystal glass.

The Water Province

The province of Västergötland, near the western coast of Sweden, has 450 kilometres of coast around the lakes Vättern and Vänern, and boarders the Kattegat. As if that was not enough, the Göta Älv, Sweden's greatest river by volume, runs through the province. When the sluices are opened, 300,000 litres of water pour down every second. Generally, water and fishing are two key words for this area!

Vänern is Europe's third greatest lake with a total area of 5,900 square kilometres. It also has a lovely archipelago which receives up to 2,000 hours of sun every year. In prehistoric times Vänern was a bay forming part of the sea, it was slowly cut off and formed into a lake. Some of the fish species from the sea still exist in the lake today. As much as 1,300 tonnes of fish are caught in these waters every year – mainly salmon, whitefish and pikeperch.

Another magnificent wildlife experience is the dancing cranes of Hornborga Lake. In April each year this spectacle is watched by as many as 80,000 visitors. Thousands of cranes come to the lake to perform their mating dance. Whilst trumpeting loudly the birds bend, circle around each other and take lively steps to show their affection. The whole scene is truly something out of the ordinary.

PHOTO: HANS NELSÄTER/BILDARKIVET

The elk is very common in central Sweden.

Magical Värmland

Close to Lake Vänern lies the province of Värmland, known for its deep forests and distinguished cultural figures. The village names of Värmland often incorporate the nature of the spot – brook, valley, rapid, forest or ridge. It is the differences between the highlands and lowland which create the striking beauty of this area.

The Nobel Prize winner Selma Lagerlöf is one of the authors associated with Värmland. The Lagerlöf family farm, Mårbacka, is open to the public. She found material for her books in this native district, even though she usually changed the names of the farms and places. In the library one can find almost all the translations of her works.

Finns have put their distinctive mark on this area. In the beginning of the 17th century poverty drove many Finns to emigrate. Quite a few of them arrived in Värmland, where they worked in the woods. Certain parts have retained their Finnish heritage and culture. Some farms have been preserved with furniture, saunas and equipment from olden days.

Wooden churches are also part of the Värmland landscape. One of the more famous is the Södra Råda Church, which was built around the year 1300. With its wood shingle roof and walls, it is the only example of its kind today. The chancel received its rich gothic decorations in 1323 and the legends and biblical motifs were painted a hundred years later.

Fishing and Seaside Resorts
Just north of Västergötland, close to the Norwegian border, lies Bohuslän. The history and destiny of this province is very much connected with the sea. The Kattegat and the Skagerrak have always been essential for communications and fishing.

To the memory of the seafarers of the Bronze Age, the coasts are filled with mounds of stones, which have guided sailors for more than 3,000 years. The abundance of ancient fortresses shows that the paths to the Western Seas had to be defended. One of those is the Bohus Fortress, which was built in the 14th century.

The fishing villages of Bohuslän have, over time, become more scarcely populated and have changed character, but during each summer they come

Village in the west coast archipelago.

alive again. During the last two centuries the seaside resorts have played an important role for this province as well. Two of the oldest ones are Gustafsberg and Uddevalla, during the first half of the 19th century many famous personalities visited there with their families to enjoy salt, seaweed or mud baths.

Smögen is the biggest fishing community in Bohuslän, where the fishing fleet unloads its catch and the daily shrimp auction takes place. Today, it is also a seaside resort with an international atmosphere. "Ströget", the kilometre long wooden boardwalk by the quay, is an impressive promenade with colourful boathouses and visiting vessels.

The Heart of Sweden

For most Swedes, Dalarna, the province in the heart of the country, means Midsummer, fiddlers, white birches and the maidens of the famous artist Zorn. However, this landscape also stands for the wealth of the earth. For several centuries the Falun Mine has been a cornerstone of the Swedish economy.

The Falun Mine has been exploited since the end of the 11th century. Copper, gold, silver, sulphur, sulphuric acid and the famous red paint of Falun are products from this mine. The red paint is a by-product, which is used to paint houses and has become a national symbol.

A 60 kilometre long route of culture and nature called Husbyringen has been created in Dalarna. Here the visitor can experience both ancient and modern times. Along the path lies the Husby Royal Mansion, where the Dala-law was established in the 13th century. The nearby church houses many items from the Middle Ages. The next stop might be the Stjärnsund Mansion, built by the inventor Christopher Polhem and his partner in 1699. Here Polhem invented machines, manufactured tools and clocks and constructed all kinds of equipment. Christopher Polhem has been called the Father of Swedish Mechanics. A final visit might include the site of the Gudsberga Monastery, the Catholic Church's most northern outpost in the country. It was built in 1486 and closed in 1527 by King Gustav Vasa. Excavations have revealed parts of the building, some coins and fragments of a saintly image.

Idyllic Islands

sun, winds and natural life

The mythical island Gotland is renowned for its different landscape. The characteristic stonewalls, the impressive rauks (stones sculptured by the sea), the barren heaths and the snow-white beaches all blessed with a sunny climate, make it an ideal place for a vacation. With its 50,000 sheep and its quarrying, the island is also very active in trade and industry. Another interesting side of Gotland is its ancient history. Archaeologists have discovered that the island may have been inhabited during the Stone Age. From the Viking Age alone, 700 treasures have been found.

The first people came to Gotland about 8,000 years ago. The sea has always been the most important source for food for the islands inhabitants. Many stone paintings of ships from the Bronze Age have been discovered. Numerous silver treasures bear witness to Gotland being a centre for Baltic sea trade in the Viking Age. The island has been part of Sweden since 1645 having previously been under Danish and German rule at various times.

An old fary tale from the 13th century tells that Gotland was an enchanted island, which sank during daytime and rose again at night. The enchantment was broken when a man called Tjelvar came to the island and built a fire. The old story has been verified by geological research! In prehistoric times the island did rise and fall, and this can be seen by examining the beach embankments, which extend to the island's highest parts.

Gotland's beautiful capital Visby has been included in UNESCO's World Heritage list, which means that it will be preserved for future generations. It is "an extraordinary example of a northern European ring-walled Hansa city, which in a unique way has kept its original form". Its ring wall was built 700 years ago and is still much the same today. The irregular residential blocks with narrow houses and small alleys remain intact and the giant warehouses remind the visitor of the immense wealth collected there during medieval times.

Another picturesque island is Öland, which is Sweden's second largest island and its smallest province. It is often referred to as the "Island of sun and wind" and has over 2,000 windmills. The limestone subsoil and special

The extraordinary landscape of Öland, "Stora Alvaret".

The ancient ring wall of Visby on Gotland.

climate have given the island a very rich flora with an abundance of rare species. Plants from Siberia, the Alps and Eastern Europe have survived the Ice Age and warmer post-glacial periods. No less than 30 different species of orchids exist on the island.

The extraordinary area "Stora Alvaret" on southern Öland consists of a treeless, forty kilometres long plain, with limestone outcrops. This landscape is considered unique to northern Europe. However, around Borgholm, the capital city, the terrain is entirely different. Here we find the largest forest of deciduous trees in southern Sweden. Öland is also an island of many beaches – grass-covered in the south and sandy in the north! Statistically, Öland is the province with the most hours of sun and least rainfall.

Solliden, the Royal Family's summer residence, is situated three kilometres from Borgholm. The castle was built for the Swedish Queen Victoria in 1903–1906. Most of the park contains its original vegetation, but there is a Dutch rose garden and many trees with varieties rare in these latitudes.

For those who are interested in birds, the Ottenby bird observatory is worth a visit. This station is Sweden's oldest and largest, and is considered one of the most important in Europe. Seven scientists work here and are engaged in approximately twenty research projects monitoring the migration of birds.

Northern Sweden

land of the Midnight Sun

Lapland is the northernmost and largest province of Sweden, covering some 109,702 square kilometres of wilderness and natural beauty, most of which lies above the Arctic Circle. Its mountain chain was formed 425 million years ago when the continental plates of Europe and North America collided.

The Samis (or Lapps) have inhabited northern Europe since ancient times and constitute a minority group linguistically, culturally and demographically. Formerly, they were a nomadic people, living principally by hunting and fishing. Today the remaining 15,000 Lapps mostly have other occupations, but some still work by herding reindeer. In the whole area of Lapland there are five Sami villages which during a year produce 500 tons of reindeer meat.

These natives of the North have a very rich culture. In Ájtte, a museum of the Samic culture and religion has been built, exhibiting their fine handicraft and history.

PHOTO: WÄSTFELTS, JOKKMOKK

A Laplander and his reindeer.

Popular Pastimes

The Swedish mountains stretch from central Sweden to the country's northern border. There is a rich variety of skiing tracks and trails and slopes for all types of skiers. Some slopes open as early as October, and you can ski until the end of April in places such as Åre, and until June in the far north. There you can also enjoy the northern lights – or aurora borealis – which have fascinated man through the ages. They are a nocturnal light phenomenon seen in the polar areas in winter. The sky is filled with light rays in the form of bows, beams and curtains. This is caused by "solar flares", where the sun erupts and electrically charged particles are thrown out into the ionosphere.

Jig fishing is another popular pastime in northern Sweden. You drill a hole in the ice of a lake and drop your line into the cold water below. If you are lucky, you can catch a char weighing up to 1.5 kilos! Fishing is very popular in Sweden and it has been estimated that up to 2.2 million Swedes take part in this sport every year.

Exploiting Ore

Northern Sweden has always been connected with mining. In the 17th century attempts were made to extract the ore from the Lapland Mountains. The breakthrough for ore exploitation was the arrival of the possibility of transporting it by train. Previously, the ore had been transported along small paths by Lapps and their reindeer.

An interesting site is the Underground Church in Kristineberg. In 1946 a two metre high Christlike figure appeared on the rock-face of the mine. Today, some 50 years later, the unique St. Anna Church occupies the very same spot, ninety metres below the surface of the earth.

Trekking

For those who enjoy trekking, the North is a paradise. "The King's Route" is a marked path through the Swedish mountains. It has small cottages and rest stations on the route, all the way from Abisko, via Kebnekaise and Saltoluokta, down to Kvikkjokk. During the walk, you will see waterfalls, breathtaking canyons and unforgettable mountain scenery.

Sweden's highest mountain, Kebnekaise, is situated in Lapland. In this wild area over twenty mountain peaks extend to over 1,700 metres and there are at least fifteen glaciers. The nearby Tarfala Valley, which is unique in its barren beauty, is the site of a research station for glacier studies.

One of this mountainous area's best-known sights is the "Lap Gateway", with its broad opening towards the Abisko Valley. Abisko is a national park and the King's Route begins here. The largest national park in Sweden is situated in Padjelanta by the Lule River, and covers over 2,050 square kilometres. It is an open, wide plain with a few mountain peaks. The lake Virihaure is renowned for its scenery. In 1731, during his travels in Lapland the famous botanist Carl von Linné described the area's rich flora. At Staloluokta, a traditional Samic camp is built, huts with bunks, a church tepee and a tourist centre for the traveller's enjoyment.

Norrbotten

The thinly populated northern province of Norrbotten meets the Finnish border along two rivers. The wild, game-rich interior made the area a suitable place for settlement when man hunted to survive. The rivers were teeming with salmon.

Kukkola is a fascinating site in Norrbotten. It is an old fishing and milling settlement by the Torne River. Today, Kukkola has a Fishing Museum worth seeing, and in the rapid you can try the traditional fishing method used when catching whitefish with bag nets on a long pole. The highlight of the whitefish season is at the end of July, when people gather to grill and eat the freshly caught fish.

Storforsen, the Great Falls, is Scandinavia's largest natural waterfall and a designated nature reserve. The Pite River, one of the few main rivers that has not been developed for hydroelectric generation, has a stretch of rapids approximately five kilometres long. Storforsen is the last two kilometres, where the river drops an amazing sixty metres. Stone breakwaters were built centuries ago to divert the current. This has resulted in the Dead Fall, a gigantic dry area with giant "pots" and flat rocks. Just upstream one can find a Forestry Museum, including forest huts from different periods, tar burning and charcoals stacks and a raftsman's hut.

Stockholm

Venice of the north

The capital of Sweden, Stockholm, has often been called one of the world's most beautiful capital cities. The city is surrounded by the Stockholm archipelago, which consists of an amazing 24,000 islands and skerries, and it is situated by Lake Mälaren. With its 1.6 million inhabitants, Greater Stockholm is Sweden's principal industrial city and second port.

The city is built partly on fourteen islands, linked by bridges spanning glistening expanses of water. The accessibility is very good because of the excellent public transport system. Stockholm is considered to be a very safe city, and a clean one – its inhabitants have pledged for it to become Europe's cleanest city!

Stockholm is mentioned as a city for the first time in a document of 1252, and it had a "capital" designation from this time. Around the reign of Gustav II Adolf, the city became the centre of politics and grew in population and area. The first city planning regulation was made in the 17th century. The name itself originally referred to the name of the main island, Stadsholmen. The word "Stock" (log) might refer to the logs which formed a bridge over Norrström. "Holm" means islet.

A wealth of cultural attractions is to be found in Stockholm, there are over 70 museums, 100 galleries and 70 theatres. One can find something for every taste and interest. The most famous museum is probably that of the Vasa, with its magnificent 17th century warship, salvaged after 333 years at the bottom of the sea. The ship sank on its maiden voyage just off Stockholm. Today it stands in the largest covered ship museum in the world.

The baroque-inspired Royal Palace is another essential place to visit. It houses many exhibits, such as the Royal Armoury, the Royal Treasury and the Royal Apartments, with their splendid interiors. Today, the Royal Family lives just outside the city, in the 17th century Drottningholm Palace, a popular accessible attraction for all. The Drottningholm Theatre is also situated here, with its original 18th century stage settings. Every summer operas and concerts are performed here.

The Old Town ("Gamla Stan") has become one of Stockholm's famous attractions. Its narrow streets, old signs and medieval atmosphere are something quite special. This area is home to many artisans, who have their workshops and studios in the neighbourhood. There is also plenty of good food to be found in the Old Town.

Skansen, the world's oldest open-air museum, is another essential visit. It features 150 buildings of historical and cultural significance from all over Sweden and its zoo also includes most animals that are to be seen in Sweden; reindeer, elk, wolves etc. There is a replica 18th century district with various kinds of workshops.

Stockholm is an eldorado for the nature lover. One third of Stockholm's city area is water, one third residential and commercial developments and the remaining third comprises parks and woodlands!

Within the city limits and surroundings there are undisturbed woods and meadowlands. The first urban national park, the Royal Ecopark, offers rarely found fauna and flora and a large number of culturally important buildings.

The archipelago is rich in nature. Birka, an island in Lake Mälaren, is easily reached by boat from Stockholm. During the Viking Era, it was the most important trading centre in Sweden. Excavations were carried out in 1995 and numerous artefacts were found.

In conclusion, Stockholm by night is a world bustling with activities. Nightclubs, restaurants, concerts, theatres, cafés, the list is endless. Today, Stockholm has more restaurants per capita than most other European cities. Even in the 18th century there were some 700 inns – one for every 100 inhabitants! The visitor should take the opportunity to taste traditional Swedish cooking; herring, salmon, reindeer and bleak roe.

PHOTO: HANS NELSÄTER/BILDARKIVET

Drottningholm, home of the Royal Family.

PHOTO: ERIK G SVENSSON/PRESSENS BILD

Skating during winter in downtown Stockholm.

Recipes

Today, food from all parts of the world can be found in Sweden. Younger people, especially, prefer foreign food to Swedish traditional cooking.

Still, many households cook and eat typical home-cooked dishes, "husmanskost". Many of these dishes are included in the famous "smörgåsbord".

In the following pages we guide you through some of the culinary traditions that Sweden offers today.

Fried Baltic Herring
4 servings

1 kg Baltic herring

½ tablespoon salt

For the coating:

1 egg

100 g sifted breadcrumbs

Clean the fish, cut off the fins, but leave the back bone. Rinse and salt the herring. Flatten the filets.

Dip them in egg and turn them in the breadcrumbs.

Fry the herring until they look crunchy.

Serve them with mashed potatoes, sour cream, minced red onion and chive.

PHOTO: FREDRIK REGE, STYLIST: ULRICA NORBERG

Stuffed Cabbage Rolls

6 servings

Strip the outside leaves from the cabbage and cut out the stalk. Put the whole cabbage in to boiling salted water and let it boil until the leaves are a little soft and starting to come off. Remove them one by one. Mix the mashed potatoes with the mince. Add the breadcrumbs mixed with the milk, and season the mixture.

Put about 1 tablespoon of the mixture on every cabbage leaf and make them into small packets (rolls).

Brown a few cabbage rolls at a time, add the golden syrup on top and move them to a meat roaster.

When all the rolls have been browned, you mix in the cabbage liquid and stock and let the rolls fry slowly for 45 minutes to 1 hour depending on the freshness of the cabbage.

Thicken the meat juice to make a gravy. Put the rolls in a bowl and pour the sauce on top.

Serve with boiled potatoes and lingonberry jam.

1 average-sized white cabbage

500 g finely minced beef

2 boiled potatoes

50 g golden breadcrumbs

50–100 ml milk

salt

pepper

2–3 tablespoons butter

½ tablespoon golden syrup

cabbage liquid and stock

PHOTO: FREDRIK REGE, STYLIST: ULRICA NORBERG

Meatballs

6 servings

Mix the breadcrumbs with milk and leave to soak for a while. Mash the potatoes. Put the meat in a bowl, season it lightly and add the potatoes. Thereafter add the breadcrumb mix little by little and add the onion. Stir in the whipped egg. Taste the meat carefully. Form the meat into round balls. Brown the meatballs until they are golden.

Serve them with boiled potatoes, lingonberry jam and pickled gherkins.

500 g minced meat (more beef than pork)

salt

pepper

2 boiled potatoes

75 g golden breadcrumbs

200 ml milk

2 tablespoons minced onion, browned

1 egg

PHOTO: FREDRIK REGE, STYLIST: ULRICA NORBERG

Jansson's Temptation

6 servings

Jansson's Temptation belongs to the "smörgåsbord". Clean the anchovies or slice the fillets. Peel and slice the potatoes into large matchstick-sized pieces. Put the potatoes into cold water (to keep from discolouring). Peel the onion, slice it and brown it slightly in some of the butter. Grease an ovenproof dish thoroughly. Dry the potato sticks in a cloth. Place a layer of potato in the dish then the anchovy and onions. Repeat these layers.

6–10 Swedish anchovies or 12–20 small fillets

6–8 average-sized raw potatoes

2–4 yellow or red onions

2–3 tablespoons butter or margarine

2 tablespoons breadcrumbs

250–300 ml cream or milk

Put the remainder of the potatoes on top and cover with breadcrumbs. Dice the remaining butter over it. Bake the dish in a hot oven (225–250 °C) until the potatoes are golden. Pour over the cream. Bake for a further 50–60 minutes or until the potatoes are soft.

PHOTO: FREDRIK REGE, STYLIST: ULRICA NORBERG

Reindeer "skav" with Chanterelles

2–3 servings

250 g reindeer meat in slices (skav)

1 yellow onion

2 hg fresh chanterelles

Defrost the reindeer meat somewhat. Fry the chanterelles in butter in a frying pan. Slice the peeled onion and brown it with butter. Collect the onion and fry the reindeer meat. Add the chanterelles and onion. Dilute with some water and spice with salt and black pepper. Let it simmer for about five minutes. Serve with mashed potatoes and garnish with parsley.

PHOTO: HENRIK SCHRÖDER

Pickled Herring

The fillets may need to lie in water for 24 hours. Boil water, vinegar essence and sugar. Let the fluid cool off. Cut the fillets diagonally in 2 cm pieces. Put the herring in a well-cleaned glass jar which closes well. Clean the leek and cut it in half centimetre shreds. Peel the onions and slice them thinly. Crush the peppercorns. Put the leek, onion, pepper and bay leafs on the herring fillets. Pour the cold fluid over the herring and let it rest at least 24 hours in the refrigerator before you serve it or flavour it further.

8 watered down herring fillets

300 ml water

150 ml vinegar essence, 12 %

200 ml sugar

1 leek

2 red onions

4 bay leafs

20 peppercorns

PHOTO: HENRIK SCHRÖDER

Ginger Snaps

150 pieces

Pour syrup and butter into a saucepan. Heat until it melts. Add whipping cream and spices and stir. Pour into a bowl. Add bicarbonate with some of the flour and mix into the dough. Add the rest of the flour. Work the dough and let it rest over night. Turn on the oven at 200 °C. Roll out the dough thinly on a floured baking table and cut out the snaps with measures. Put them on baking sheets with butter and bake in the middle of the oven for about five minutes. Let the gingers snaps cool on the sheets.

150 ml dark syrup

300 ml sugar

200 g butter

150 ml whipping cream

1 tablespoon ground ginger

1 tablespoon ground cinnamon

½ tablespoon ground cloves

½ tablespoon ground cardamom

1 tablespoon bicarbonate

1,1 litre flour

PHOTO: BO INGVAR JÖNSSON

Semlor
(Cream buns eaten during lent)

30 small buns

Melt the butter, add milk and heat to 37 °C (finger warm). Crumble the yeast in a bowl. Pour milk into it. Stir until the yeast has dissolved. Add salt, cottage cheese, cardamom, sugar and most of the flour. Work the dough until it is firm. Ferment under a towel about 30 minutes. Turn on the oven at 250 °C. Work the dough on a floured baking table and make small, round buns. Put them on baking sheets and let them ferment for 20 minutes. Cover them in beat-up egg. Bake in the middle of the oven for 5–7 minutes. Let the buns cool under a towel. Cut a small lid on each bun and take out some of the bread inside the bun. Mix it with grated marzipan and milk. Fill the buns with the mix. Whip the cream and dab it on the buns. Put the lids back on and sift some powdered sugar on top.

50 g butter

250 ml milk

25 g yeast

125 ml cottage cheese

2 pinches ground cardamom

75 ml sugar

800–900 ml wheatflour

1 beat-up egg

Filling:

200 g almond paste (marzipan)

100 ml milk

250 ml whipping cream

powdered sugar

The Swedish Schnapps

traditional drink for every occasion

According to tradition schnapps, or aquavit, is part of the Swedish Christmas, Easter, Midsummer and Crayfish table. It has become very much part of the Swedish culinary tradition.

PHOTO: FREDRIK REGE, STYLIST: ULRICA NORBERG

Skål! (Cheers!)

It is also acceptable to drink schnapps before eating. It may sound strange, but the schnapps will "awaken" the taste buds and then you can taste the delicious food better. You can also use the schnapps to heighten the flavour of the main course.

How does one drink schnapps the right way? Traditionally it is drunk ice-cold, in one fell swoop, often accompanied by one of many hundreds of drinking songs. If you cannot drink it down in one, you are allowed to "cut in half".

Below you will find the basic recipe for spiced schnapps:

Buy vodka with 30–33 % alcohol and decide which spices you will use (for example aniseed, dill or caraway).

Blend and make as much as you want and leave it for 14 days at room temperature. Put in a closed container so that the alcohol does not evaporate. After 14 days, filter through, for example, a coffee filter. Pour it back in a bottle. Leave for at least another two weeks. Enjoy it and experience the different spices!